Explaining
The
Church

Colin Dye

Sovereign World

ISBN: 1 85240 161 3

SOVEREIGN WORLD LIMITED
P.O. Box 777, Tonbridge, Kent TN11 9XT, England.

Typeset and printed in the UK by Sussex Litho Ltd, Chichester, West Sussex.

Contents

Introduction

I am sure you agree that we must go on reading and re-reading the New Testament if we want the church to grow, mature and carry on being renewed by God's Spirit.

Many leaders suggest, however, that the New Testament does not offer us a pattern for the Church, and argue that its teaching is not applicable today. They maintain that [i] the New Testament church existed in a different culture and age; [ii] it was a baby church which did not mature for several centuries; and [iii] it followed a special pattern which was only for the time of the foundation apostles.

Some leaders insist that the New Testament church sets a rigid pattern of structure and practice which must be applied today in every small detail. Other leaders select whatever seems helpful from the New Testament teaching about the church: they pick and choose those ideas which seem to work best. For myself, I think that the New Testament reveals basic principles about the church which can be applied in every age and culture.

I am convinced that the New Testament is the perfect manual for every aspect of church life and management. Yet I am equally sure that the New Testament principles are meant to be applied in different ways in different cultures. We must follow the principles, but – with the Spirit's help – we should vary the details to fit our situation and culture.

I have written this booklet to help us understand the church. If we are to do this, we need to lay aside our own ideas and let God speak to us about his church through his Scriptures. We live at a time when congregations are growing and multiplying with increasing speed; so it is surely vital that we establish this growth on biblical principles – rather than on human ideas and traditions.

In this booklet, I am not trying to explain principles about today's churches. Rather, I am setting out some of the more important New Testament principles about the church. Once we have a biblical understanding of the church, we can follow the principles and – relying on the Spirit's help to apply them in our locality – take steps to move towards a more biblical church.

I pray that this booklet will help fan renewal and prepare the church for revival. Please understand that our secular generation will be challenged only by a radical church which is truly biblical.

Colin Dye
Kensington Temple
May 1996

1

What Is
The Church?

As evangelical Christians, we are generally aware that the Bible does not mean a building when it refers to the church. Yet when we imagine 'church' many of us still tend to think primarily of a meeting or a denomination. Yet these views are just as traditional and non-biblical as stained-glass windows and spires! We must go back to the New Testament to understand the church.

Important Features
From studying the NT, it seems to me that the church has about ten important features. [There is not enough space in this booklet to set out scripture passages. So please read each reference in your own Bible before moving on.]

1. The church exists to bring glory to God by Christ Jesus (Ephesians 3:20-21). The church is not an end in itself; its purpose is beyond itself.

2. The church belongs to Jesus Christ; it is his church (Matthew 16:18; Acts 20:28). There is no such thing as my, our or your church. The church belongs only to Jesus.

3. The church is God-planned and God-made; it is not a human invention or social institution (Ephesians 1:4,5,11; Ephesians 2:10).

4. Christ is the head of the church (Ephesians 1:22; Colossians 1:18). No man or woman is the ultimate church leader; the church belongs to him and only he is in absolute control.

5. The church consists of members of Christ's body (1 Corinthians 12:27; Ephesians 1:22-23). Only genuine believers are part of the church – it does not contain people who are nominally Christian.

6. The church has a supernatural nature (1 Corinthians 12:13; Ephesians 2:16). By the cross and the Spirit, it is a supernatural entity – one body – which transcends time, race, status and gender.

7. The church is called to make, mobilise and mature disciples (Matthew 28:18-20). It's rightly been said that 'the church exists for mission in the same way that a fire exists for burning.' It has been charged by its head to make, baptise and teach disciples.

8. The church reaches out to the whole world (Matthew 28:19; Mark 16:15; Romans 1:16; 1 John 2:2; Revelation 5:9-10; 7:9). The church is not limited to one generation, social group, or race. It is for all people of every age and status in all nations.

9. There is only one true church. (Ephesians 4:3-6, 15-16). There is one body which is the mystical union of all genuine believers – all those alive on earth and those already in heaven.

10. The church is growing into maturity (Ephesians 4:12-13). The church is not static; it is being moulded by the Spirit into spiritual maturity.

These foundation principles mean that we can, perhaps, helpfully define the church like this. 'The Church of Jesus Christ is the supernatural fellowship and union of all God's people called for the glory of God, under the headship of Christ, to the world-wide work of making, mobilising and maturing disciples'.

Holding firm to these foundation principles, we can now move on to the two key words which the New Testament uses to describe the church.

Gathered Together – *Ekklesia*

Ekklesia is the Greek word used in the New Testament for church. It literally means 'the called out ones', but the emphasis behind the word is on gathering together. The NT's use of *ekklesia* suggests that the church has been called out of the world to be gathered together in a relationship with Christ.

This gathering can be seen when believers meet for worship, but it does not end there. All genuine believers, alive and dead, have been permanently gathered together by the cross and by the Spirit in union with each other and with Christ. So it is as important to express church or *ekklesia* out in society as in a building or Christian meeting.

In ancient Greece, the *ekklesia* was the electorate of a city. A herald summoned all the free men to the council where they would debate and vote. This calling and gathering was the assembly or *ekklesia*. The NT adopted this picture for the church.

In the Greek version of the Old Testament, the congregation of Israel was also called the *ekklesia*. Acts 7:38 refers to Israel as the church in the wilderness. God had delivered the Jews from slavery for a purpose – to be his special people, a treasured possession, who lived in loving obedience.

By the time of the New Testament, *ekklesia* was a familiar term for God's people. It suggested the idea that God was preparing a people who would bring him glory and through whom he could show his love and grace.

Ekklesia is used in the NT in three main ways to describe [i] the Universal Church, [ii] a local church, and [iii] a household church. Each of these uses of *ekklesia* is valid on its own, but a complete picture of the church can be seen only by grasping all three uses.

The Universal Church

This consists of all genuine Christians everywhere – on earth and in heaven – so no church gathering on earth can rightly be considered the Universal Church. It is invisible and has no expression of its own. Instead it is expressed through *all* local and household churches.

A Local Church

In the New Testament, this consists of all the believers in any locality – like a town, city or rural area. A NT local church does *not* correspond with what is commonly called a local church today.

Modern local churches are usually smaller units of *ekklesia* than the church of an urban or rural region. They often function independently of most other churches in their locality. This was not so in the NT, when all churches in a region joined and co-operated together as the church in that locality.

A Household Church

Households were larger in New Testament times and were seen as communities in their own right, so churches naturally developed within these social structures. There were no formal church buildings then, so homes were the obvious place for believers to meet.

There seem to have been fully functioning churches expressing *ekklesia*, having leadership, and doing everything that churches should do. They were not independent units but interdependent parts of the largest local church. Quite possibly, local church leadership was drawn from household church leaders.

In the New Testament, believers were identified as part of the local church – the church in Ephesus, Corinth and so on. But some of these churches were enormous and would themselves have consisted of many different congregations or households. So today's local congregations are closer to household churches than to the other NT expressions of e*kklesia.*

All this underlines that there is no single complete expression of the Universal Church on earth. Instead there are many earthly expressions of Christ's church. However, these dare not be exclusive, separate or independent – for they are joined to Christ and, through him, are joined to each other.

This means that every expression of the One Church must consider itself to be actively interdependent with all other expressions of *ekklesia* and co-dependent with them on Christ.

Principles of *Ekklesia*

No New Testament church was merely an informal collection of Christians. Although relationship is at the heart of *ekklesia*, a NT church was more than informal fellowship in a large meeting or home. There seem to me to be four basic NT principles which have to operate before a group of believers can be considered a church.

1. Leadership is vital for e*kklesia*. Any body must have form and function, and leadership must be present in church life. Christ is The Leader, and he delegates to his under-leaders the responsibility for the spiritual care and well-being of his members. Leaders should direct according only to the spiritual authority and gifting they receive from Christ.

2. To be a genuine expression of *ekklesia*, a group must accept the complete charge that Christ has given to the church. Groups which meet for one or two purposes – like evangelism, healing or fellowship – cannot be truly called churches. Church means doing *everything!*

3. There cannot be an identifiable church without identified members. NT believers were members of a household church *and* a local church *and* the Universal Church. Leaders are called to equip members for ministry; this is impossible without some form of visible and active membership.

4. A church is not an isolated group of believers cut off from the rest of Christ's body. There is only One Church, so each expression of the church is part of the body and in partnership with all other parts. Inter-church unity and co-operation are vital for any credible expression of *ekklesia*. This partnership must be at local, national and global levels – and it must not be restricted to denominational or other emphasis boundaries. Every part of Christ's body needs all the other parts if Christ is to be expressed fully to the world.

The Challenge of *Ekklesia*

It seems to me that these New Testament principles challenge many different attitudes and practices which are common in today's churches. I have picked out three that we need to work through carefully if we are to reach a biblical understanding of the church.

Buildings

Even though most Christians know that the church is not the building, many still behave as if the building is the heart of the church. Too often, what occurs in the building is all there is to their church.

I believe that building-bound thinking restricts the church. A building's size, shape and structure can limit and hinder activities. Any church whose vision is governed by its building is hardly a NT church. We do need buildings for many church activities, but they are mere tools which should neither be reverenced nor allowed to replace the church's real identity. Remember, the dynamic early church had no purpose-built church buildings, and many of the fast-growing churches in today's developing world do not have impressive or extravagant buildings.

Meetings

Some evangelical Christians confuse church with meetings. The more meetings they have, the more they feel that they have fulfilled the church's purpose. But if church is limited to meetings, the church ceases to be when the meeting ends – and that is exactly how many Christians behave. When they leave the meeting (or the building), they feel that they have left the church until next time.

But we are not *ekklesia* because we meet, instead we meet because we are *ekklesia*. Church is both an eternal relationship and a series of earthly responsibilities. Most churches lose power and vitality when their life and mission are formalised mainly in meetings.

Organisations

The church is a living organism which owes its life to God and not to human organisation. Obviously organisation (like buildings and meetings) has a role in working out *ekklesia*, but – like them – it should not be central.

I believe that excessive organisation leads to unhelpful methods, a confusion of goals and cumbersome structures. Institutional goals can replace spiritual aims. Commercial motives and secular practices often creep in. Ambition replaces service. Hierarchical leadership structures are borrowed from business life. Over-organisation slowly squeezes life and flexibility from the church.

Denominations are human organisations which are meant to facilitate God's work. There is a place for them, but they must be flexible and open to the Spirit; they must not control people or be controlled by people. Each individual expression of *ekklesia* must be led by Christ, not by an organisation. *Ekklesia* – the highest example of God's will on earth – should be served and facilitated by organisation, not dominated or manipulated.

Sharers Together – *Koinonia*

The Greek word for fellowship, *koinonia*, is the second key word that the New Testament uses in relation to church. *Koinonia* means sharing together with a clear common purpose. As Christians we share together in the things of God – this is the fellowship, or communion, of saints.

Like *ekklesia, koinonia* refers to the relationship we have – by the cross and by the Spirit – with God and with each other. Some believers consider *koinonia* to be one of the church's activities – what happens at the end of the services. But fellowship encircles everything that we have, are and do as believers. It is another word for church – which is why some churches refer to themselves as 'The Fellowship'.

The Basis of *Koinonia*

All genuine fellowship is founded in Christ. All that we share together as Christians we share in Jesus: he is the one in whom we are and whom we have in common. And all true fellowship is accomplished by the Holy Spirit – who is himself the Spirit of fellowship. Through the Spirit, we participate in the Son; and, through the Spirit, we are in relationship with all other believers who live in him.

Through the Word

Fellowship begins, according to 1 John 1:2-3, with the revelation of God through his Son, the Word of life. The apostles passed on the good news that Jesus came to reveal the Father perfectly and to enable us to have fellowship with the Father. We shared in their revelation of the good news when we received their message – and so fellowship began.

This fellowship is not based on intellectual agreement, but in a knowledge – an experience – of truth (1 John 5:20). Our fellowship with the living Word, with Jesus, is drawn from the written Word, the Bible. This is also the food of our fellowship with each other as we encourage and challenge one another by its teaching.

Through the Cross

We know that our sins separated us from God and that Jesus died to make fellowship with God possible. The cross establishes the basis for fellowship between God and humanity, and between people in the church (Ephesians 2:13-18; 1 John 1:7; 4:10).

These verses show that it is impossible to separate fellowship with God from fellowship with each other. The cross accomplished for humanity both a new vertical and a new horizontal relationship.

Through the Spirit

The well-known words of the grace (2 Corinthians 13:14) remind us that the Holy Spirit also produces and sustains our fellowship. He is the Spirit of fellowship and he brings us an understanding of the truth and assurance of our relationship with God.

Because – individually – we are in him and he is in us, the Spirit shares the presence, power and purity of God with us. But because all believers are in him *together*, he unites us as God's people and enables us to share together in him and in our blessings in Christ.

The Expression of *Koinonia*

Acts 2:42 describes how the first converts devoted themselves to the fellowship, to *koinonia*. This does not mean the informal aspects of church life – the bits before and after meetings. *Koinonia* is, by definition, purposeful and includes *everything* that we are called to do together as Christians. This is why Acts 2:42 identifies the church as *the* fellowship. The new converts were not devoted to informal conversations but to sharing together in a dynamic, purposeful body.

True fellowship can only be expressed within a body which is clear about its identity, purpose and function. Any believer who is not fully part of a local expression of the church is seriously remiss in their relationship with Christ. So too, any congregation which is not in full fellowship with the other nearby local expressions is equally negligent in its relationship with the head of the church.

Fellowship is expressed in obvious ways like prayer, worship, mission and ministry, but I want to highlight four other ways that the Bible teaches we evidence our fellowship.

The Lord's Supper
Holy Communion – the Lord's Supper – is a vital expression of our fellowship. It is God's specially ordained way of confirming our continuing fellowship with Christ in his blood and our continuing fellowship with each other in his body (1 Corinthians 10:16-17). Paul's practical teaching on spiritual gifts, the body

and great love is set in the context of his instructions for the Lord's Supper (1 Corinthians 11:17 – 14:40). In the NT church, the regular communion meal visibly expressed all these aspects of fellowship.

Giving to the Poor

We have seen that true fellowship, genuine *koinonia*, is sharing together, and this must have a practical expression. Because we share together spiritually in Christ we will want to share together materially too. True fellowship in Christ naturally leads to physical provision for those in need – as both an expression and evidence of the fellowship. Passages like 2 Corinthians 8:3; 1 Timothy 6:18; Hebrews 13:1; and 1 John 3:17 demonstrate that this generosity is precisely what God demands and expects. Anything less than lavish generosity to needy Christians is a denial of fellowship.

Supporting Christian Ministries

Paul often described the special partnership he enjoyed with the church in Philippi. The fellowship there repeatedly supported his travelling ministry with prayer and finance (Philippians 1:4-5; 4:15-19). Supporting ministries like this is an expression of fellowship. By our giving we become partners in the gospel with those who preach – and are blessed by God in return!

Enduring Suffering

We must never forget that, as Christians, we are called to suffer for Christ. Whenever we do this together, or identify with and support those who are suffering, we are expressing our fellowship in Christ. Verses like 1 Peter 4:13 and 1 Corinthians 12:26 show that being joined to Christ and his body means we are affected by whatever happens to our brothers and sisters. Genuine fellowship expresses this fact either in joy with the blessed or in tears with those who suffer.

Biblical Pictures

As well as the two Greek words *ekklesia* and *koinonia*, the New Testament also uses several word pictures to describe the church. No one picture fully represents the church, but they offer a helpful overview when taken together. I believe that each picture contains three identical emphases. [i] The essential corporate nature of the church; [ii] the relationship between God and his people; and [iii] the function that God has given to his church.

1 Peter 2:9 describes us *'a chosen people'* and 2 Corinthians 11:2 identifies us as *'the bride'*. We are people who have been carefully chosen from all other people to be the beloved bride of God's Son. God really has chosen us. His word cannot be broken. His love never fails. And we are called to an exclusive and intimate relationship with Christ. He prepares us to become clean and beautiful as we are brought to maturity in him.

1 Peter 2:9 also names us as *'a royal priesthood'*. We are to serve the king by sacrificially serving the king's people in all sorts of ways. This closely relates to the picture of the church as *'a holy temple'* in 1 Corinthians 3:16. We are called to live in God's presence and to fill ourselves – God's holy temple – with the priestly sacrifices of praise and prayer.

1 Peter 2:9 then calls us *'a holy nation'*. We have been set aside for a corporate life of dedication and consecration. Our common identity in Christ supersedes our natural heritage, culture and racial origin. Our primary allegiance is to God's nation rather than to our natural nation.

Finally, 1 Peter 2:9 identifies us as *'a people belonging to God'*. We are citizens of his heaven and children of his kingdom. We are subject to his laws and directed by his Spirit. We are the Lord's.

Ephesians 1:23 describes us *'his body'*. He is our head and we are his body. We are vitally connected to him and mutually dependent with all other believers. We do his work under his direction, and each member has a unique and indispensable part to play.

Ephesians 3:15 suggests that we are *God's family*. He is our Father, Jesus is our eldest brother, and all believers are our true siblings. As our Father, God provides all we need. As brothers and sisters, we care called to love and serve each other and display the family likeness to society. As a family, we should have no fewer brothers and sisters than God has sons and daughters.

1 Peter 5:2 describes the church as *'a flock'*. We are God's sheep and Jesus is our good Shepherd. He loves, knows, guards and cares for us. We need to stay close to him and close to each other. Only isolated sheep are vulnerable.

Throughout Revelation, the church is called *'the city of God'* – a place of government, safety, comfort, beauty and harmony. Without God, the city will not be established – and this will not fully happen until the new heavenly city comes down from above. For now, we are called to live as God's city on earth, influencing society for God until the ultimate city arrives.

There are two other images in the New Testament which help us understand the church more fully. At the Last Supper, in John 15:1-5, Jesus describes himself as *'the true vine'* and his apostles as the branches. This picture helps us to appreciate our essential unity with Christ and each other. It also shows that fruitfulness can result only from remaining an intimate part of the one true vine.

Then there are several New Testament passages like Matthew 16:18-19; Ephesians 6:10-20; and 1 Peter 5:8 which show that the church has a clear military function. Although the church is never specifically named in the NT as *'an army'*, clearly Jesus expects his people to be involved actively together in spiritual warfare.

2

Belonging To
The Church

In the New Testament, belonging to Christ and belonging to his body, the church, cannot be separated. Jesus' teaching about the vine, in John 15:1-8, shows that we are automatically part of each other when we are part of him. It is impossible for us to be joined to Christ and not be joined to each other in the church. And it is equally impossible for anyone to be part of the true church if they are not joined to Christ.

Being joined, or belonging, implies a vital connection – an organic relationship – with Christ. It is not enough to be on a church membership list or to have gone through a religious ritual. These things have meaning only for those who are joined to Christ and are living in a vital relationship with him through his Spirit.

Very many people claim to believe in God and to be Christian. Yet a considerable proportion of those who profess to believe in Christ are not part of, or meaningfully involved in any church. Sadly, some of those who do attend services do not have a relationship with Jesus. As 2 Timothy 3:5 describes, they have a form of religion but deny the life-giving power of Christ.

Christian Initiation

Nominalism (being a Christian only in name) is one of the world-wide church's greatest problems – especially in Europe where there are more nominal Christians than in the rest of the world put together. This is one reason why we must ensure that we preach the gospel in all its fullness.

Jesus does offer salvation to all humanity, but he also

commands *personal repentance*. He does offer forgiveness by his grace to every man, woman and child, but it is received only through *individual faith*. In the New Testament church, both these requirements were held together and both had to be evidenced before a person was received into the church's life.

However, joining the church – becoming joined to Christ – involves more than repentance and faith. In the New Testament two more events occurred when new converts began their new life in Christ. [i] They were baptised in water; and [ii] they were filled with the Holy Spirit.

In this way, new believers began their new lives on a solid foundation and were ready to start following Christ. Through these four elements, they were fully equipped for a life of fellowship, discipleship and witness. So today, if we are to move towards a more biblical church, we need to ensure that new converts make a New Testament start to their Christian life. We should encourage them to make a biblical beginning to their Christian and church life by taking the four basic steps of Christian initiation.

Repentance

Passages like Luke 3:8; 13:3; Acts 17:30-31; and 26:20 illustrate the importance of repentance. But many Christian people are not sure what the word really means. What did Jesus expect people to do when he told them to repent? Stop sinning? Start following him? Or did he mean something rather different?

The Greek word *metanoia* – repentance – means a change of mind or a change of thinking. It is formed by joining the Greek words *meta* and *noeo*. Meta means 'after' and implies a change (as in metamorphosis); and *noeo* means 'to think' or 'to understand'. So repentance essentially means a change of understanding rather than just a change in outward behaviour. It means embracing different thoughts and a brand new way of thinking which lead to God's way of living. It means a radical change in values, attitudes and outlook. It is a change of mind and heart which leads to a radical turnabout of life. *Metanoia* means total revolution.

The New Testament call to repentance is usually a call to 'change your understanding of God' or to 'change the way that you think about God'. A changed life is the fruit of repentance; it is the natural consequence of grasping who God really is and what he has done, and appreciating his divine values.

This means that a believer's first step in Christian initiation is stopping thinking about God in their old negative ways. They start to understand and act towards him as a Father who is full of forgiveness, grace, mercy and love.

Because Paul wrote to established believers, he hardly mentions repentance. But in Romans 12:2 he shows that a Christian's behaviour should be shaped by a changed mind. Paul states that our behaviour can be modelled on the standards, values and goals of contemporary society – or it can be transformed by a changed mind. He suggests that this changed mind enables us to discern God's will for ourselves. When we start thinking like God, we are soon pre-occupied with his will rather than with the world's ways.

Belief

Faith (or belief) is the second basic step of Christian initiation. Biblical faith is a natural progression from biblical repentance, for faith means believing (or accepting) the truth about Jesus: it is acting on our new understanding of God.

Becoming a Christian is beginning a relationship with Jesus Christ. Faith involves believing that Jesus is the Son of God and that he is alive today because God the Father raised him from the dead (Romans 10:8-10).

Biblical belief – faith – means far more than intellectual assent. It is belief which is acted upon. Belief in Christ means trusting him completely. It means accepting there is nothing we can do to save ourselves (there is not even a tiny contribution that we can make) and accepting that Christ has done everything necessary to save us.

John 6:35; 20:30-31; Romans 8:32 and Ephesians 1:3 describe the extent to which a living relationship with Jesus brings every provision of salvation that God has made available in Jesus. Our faith or belief does not create forgiveness, salvation or blessing. It is God who makes them available by grace. If we believe that God and his word are true, we can accept and apply his gifts – that's faith, relying on God's grace.

Too many so-called believers think that it is *their* faith which saves them. But we are saved by *his* grace – it is all God, all his work. Our part is simply to believe that God has done everything in Jesus, to accept that there is nothing we can do, and to start living in trusting dependence on Christ (Romans 4:5; Ephesians 2:8-10).

Although belief or faith is the second step in Christian initiation, it is – like repentance – the start of an on-going, life-long process. Just as our understanding of God and his ways develops throughout our earthly life, so too we are called to go on developing our trust and reliance in Jesus. Faith is not a single act; it is a continuous life as we go on trusting him for everything.

Baptism

Baptism in water is the third step of initiation, and it seals or ratifies a new convert's commitment to Christ. It is a formal sign or evidence of faith and, therefore, follows faith. The biblical order is believe – and then be baptised. Of course, like repentance and faith, baptism does not in itself save anyone. Instead it is a public pledge to follow Christ, an oath of allegiance to the one whom we now fully trust.

But baptism is not merely something a new believer does to demonstrate faith and repentance. The New Testament makes it clear that God also acts in baptism in a clear and decisive way. The water is the sign and seal of several different spiritual actions which are accomplished by the Godhead.

The Spirit was active at Jesus' baptism, and he is associated with baptism throughout the New Testament (John 3:5; Acts 2:38; 9:17-18; 10:47; 1 Corinthians 12:13; 2 Corinthians 1:22; Ephesians 1:13; Titus 3:5). He is present at baptism, he accomplishes God's work through baptism and he is the promised gift of baptism.

God revealed Jesus as 'My Son' at his baptism, and Galatians

3:24-27 shows how our sonship is sealed in baptism. But more than this, the following spiritual blessings – all necessary for sonship – are also associated with baptism.

Acts 2:38; 22:16; Titus 3:5; and Hebrews 10:22 link baptism with forgiveness and cleansing from sin.

John 3:3-5 and Titus 3:5 demonstrate its association with new birth and kingdom entry.

Matthew 28:19; Acts 8:16; 19:5; Romans 6:1-11; 1 Corinthians 12:13 and Galatians 3:27 show that, in baptism, God signifies and seals our union with the Son, our involvement in the death and burial of Christ, and our incorporation into his body.

These baptismal blessings do not come *from* baptism; they are confirmed and sealed by God *through* baptism. In Romans 6:1-11 Paul states that the believer's unity with Christ is consummated and consolidated at baptism, but the full experience of these blessings is dependent upon a daily counting of the cost of obedient faith.

These blessings of baptism – the third step of initiation – do not operate automatically. Rather, baptism is God's public witness that he has secured or sealed these blessings for a new believer. So baptism points back to God's work on the cross and forward (as at Jesus' baptism) to a brand new life of faith.

Receiving the Spirit
The fourth and final step of initiation equips a new believer for the new life of faith. The NT uses several different phrases to describe receiving the Spirit – being filled with the Spirit, being baptised in the Spirit, being anointed with the Spirit, and being sealed with the Spirit. But whatever description is used, the NT shows that the Spirit is always given to equip the convert for effective service.

The Spirit was at work like this in the Old Testament in the lives of a few special people. But Joel 2:28-29 and Ezekiel 36:25-27 show that a time would come when he would be freely available to all believers.

In John 14:16-23, Jesus taught that the Spirit was just like him and would be sent to help all believers when he had returned to heaven. The primary role of the Spirit is to bring the presence and activity of Christ into the life of every believer (2 Corinthians 4:17-18). There is an automatic and unconscious receiving of the Spirit for every convert at the time of their new birth (Romans 8:9). But belonging to Christ involves more than just being indwelt by the Spirit, it also means being equipped for effective service.

This equipping – the fourth step – is not automatic, but is additional to the Spirit's coming at the new birth. In the NT, equipping with power for service is a definite, conscious experience which is accompanied by spiritual phenomena (Luke 24:49; Acts 1:8; 10:44-45; 11:15-17; 19:2-6). The NT church ensured that every believer had fully received the Spirit so that they could be effective witnesses for Christ (Acts 8:14-17; 9:17; 19:2). It seems to me that five NT principles are associated with this equipping.

1. The purpose of receiving the Spirit is empowering for service (Luke 24:49; John 16:7-15; Acts 1:8). The Spirit is not given for selfish or entertaining purposes, but to enable the church to reach the lost and fulfil its God-given charge.

2. The empowering or equipping is for everyone and not just a few special Christians. It is for every member of the body (Acts 2:38-39). It is for 'as many as the Lord our God will call', so it is not restricted to the NT church.

3. The equipping follows after faith. In every example in the New Testament, those who were filled/baptised/sealed/anointed with the Spirit had *already* believed. This shows that the empowering is not given automatically at new birth. NT church leaders made sure that every new believer sought the Spirit and prayed with them to receive the Spirit (Acts 8:14-17; 9:17; 19:2-6; Ephesians 1:13).

4. The equipping is a free gift. The Spirit was poured out at Pentecost and is now freely available to the church. The Spirit is a gift from God not a reward for those who are outstandingly holy

or talented (Galatians 3:2, 13-14).

5. The equipping is evidenced by tongues – a special sign of prophetic speech. People prophesied when the Spirit came upon them in the Old Testament (1 Samuel 10:10-11; 19:20-24; Numbers 11:16-30). So it should not surprise us that people spoke prophetically when they were empowered by the Spirit in the New Testament (Luke 1:41-45, 67; Acts 2:4; 10:44-47; 19:5-6). At the moment of empowering in the NT, this prophetic speech was often praise to God in unlearnt languages, in tongues. But, after the empowering, the prophetic speech was usually powerful words of witness to the risen Lord.

We have seen the four elements that the New Testament shows to be necessary for full Christian initiation into Christ and into his body, the church. But many people want to know whether they will go to heaven if they have not been baptised, or have not been empowered with the Spirit. The Bible makes it plain that we are saved by grace through faith alone. Baptism and receiving the Spirit are not conditions for entering heaven.

But joining Christ is not merely about getting a 'ticket to heaven'. It means being equipped to live with and for Jesus on earth, being his body, doing his work with his effectiveness. God wants us to receive everything he has for us and not be content with the minimum.

This is why full initiation was looked for throughout the NT whenever people turned to Christ. If we are to move towards a more biblical church, we will also ensure that every new member has an equally solid biblical foundation for their life in the church.

Church Commitment

We have seen that we become members of the church by believing in Jesus. Every true believer is automatically a member of the Universal Church. But we also know that our membership of the Universal Church must be expressed through membership of a local or household church. Local church commitment is a basic requirement for every Christian.

It is obvious that there can be no real life in the one body without church commitment – the body cannot function without committed and clearly recognised members. Church members are a work force. In Ephesians 4:11-12, church leaders are called to knit the members together and equip them for the work of ministry. Clearly this is only possible if it is clear who is committed to each local expression of the church.

The New Testament Greek phrase for church membership is *epi to auto*. This phrase first appears in Acts 1:15 'the number of believers together [*epi to auto*] was...' and implies a formally constituted body. It also appears in Acts 2:1; 2:44; and 2:47. Some leaders suggest that NT churches had no structure, and that the Holy Spirit only blesses where there is no structure to restrict him.

But people knew when they were joining the NT church and they knew when they were leaving. They did certain things when they were in the church; they were committed to each other, and came together to do certain tasks. Each fellowship was formally expressed and structured – they were not loose collections of individuals. Their members were part of a body and were held together by spiritual bonds in a cross-forged relationship. Each fellowship was part of the one body, relating in love and commitment to the other expressions of that one body.

Paul's 'body' teaching in Ephesians 4:15-16 and Colossians 2:18-19 shows that Christian commitment is indistinguishable from church commitment. Belonging to Christ means being in union with – being joined to – one body. Holding on to the head means being committed in a body relationship with all the other members of the body in the local church.

If we do not live as part of a committed local fellowship we are in danger of spiritually withering away. And if any local fellowship is not committed to all the other nearby congregations, it too is in danger of damaging the one body. No individual and no congregation can live the Christian life in isolation: there must be genuine commitment to the one body at *every* level.

We can see – both in the life of Jesus and in the early church –

that New Testament believers worked their church/Christian commitment out in four complementary ways. From the Reformation until recently, Protestants in the Western Church have mainly focused on [i] an individual response to Christ; and [ii] the congregation grouping. Believers have been expected to be committed personally to Christ and also to be part of a local congregation which exists independently of other local congregations. However, we need to appreciate that believers in the NT church expressed their commitment in a far greater variety of ways.

Companion

We know from John's gospel that the apostle John was particularly close to Jesus. He was 'the beloved disciple'. Although Jesus had his own private relationship with his Father, and had relationships with the twelve and the wider group of disciples, he also had a companion in John.

Matthew 10:1-5 describes Jesus' commissioning of the inner twelve for ministry, and it lists them in pairs: Simon and Andrew; James and John; Philip and Bartholomew; Thomas and Matthew; James and Thaddaeus; Simon and Judas. When they went out in ministry, they did not go alone. They had a companion.

Luke 10:1 records how Jesus also sent out the wider group of seventy two in pairs, and Acts shows that Paul had a series of close companions. Even in Revelation 11, there are two witnesses rather than one or a larger number.

If we are serious about understanding the church in a biblical way, we will look to finding ways of developing true companionship within the church – but not to the exclusion of any other commitments.

Cell

It is instructive that Jesus carefully chose a small group of twelve disciples whom he taught in a particularly intimate way. We also see, in Acts, that Paul usually drew a cell/team around himself who learnt from him and ministered with him. There was no fixed number for this group but it seems to have varied between three and twelve.

There are quite different dynamics in a group of this size. People can know each other well, can care practically for each other, can know that they belong and have a role. Groups of this size seem to have been the New Testament leadership pattern for training as everyone can develop their own part in Christ's ministry in a secure way.

Much of the NT teaching about the church is 'do this or that to one another'. All these different exhortations can be worked out best in a small group of this size.

Most churches have established cell groups in recent years. But too many of these have been inward looking and meeting orientated, being little more than mini mid-week services, rather than action groups that train, care and express *ekklesia* and *koinonia* in a locality.

Congregation

Once a group is larger than twelve it is hard for everyone to know each other equally well. In groups from twelve to about two hundred, there remains a level of intimacy and everybody can know each other's name and participate in some way. Groups of this size can be seen in Luke 10:1-20 and Acts 1:15 – and most NT churches would have begun at this level.

More can be done with larger congregation size groups. It is big enough to be a visible presence in the local community, but still small enough for individuals to contribute in worship along the lines of 1 Corinthians 14:26.

Celebration

Meetings become spectator orientated when groups are larger than two hundred, but the New Testament contains several examples of very large groups of people gathering to hear God's word – these are community celebrations.

Large gatherings have a special dynamic which establishes a strong corporate identity – even though very few can take part.

People are encouraged by feeling part of a larger whole, but 'church' is much more than celebration.

Jesus – our example in all things – was committed to intimate companionship with John, to twelve inner disciples, to the large group from whom the seventy two were selected, and to the crowds of thousands who wanted to hear him speak. Jesus moved with ease between all these size groups, and we can see that the early church followed his example.

There is a dynamic tension in holding these complementary commitments together – every individual feels more comfortable in one size grouping and less comfortable in another. But we do need to redress imbalances so that we develop a full experience and practice of the church.

If we want to move towards a biblical church, it is important that we rediscover these four layers of commitment both as individuals and as congregations. Without this strong commitment, the church will remain weak and divided and the world will stay unreached and unconvinced.

3

The Functioning
Church

We have seen that the New Testament considers the church to be an organism rather than an organisation. However, an organism is – according to the Oxford English dictionary – 'an organised body consisting of mutually connected and dependent parts constituted to share a common life'.

This means that the church can only function properly when every expression – individual, companion, cell, congregation and celebration – is interdependent and co-dependent on Christ. And that it can function effectively only when it has some sort of structure, government and leadership.

Before examining these things we need to remind ourselves of three important NT principles:

1. Every member of the body of Christ is ordered of God (1 Corinthians 12:18).

2. Every member of the body is mutually connected, dependent, joined and held together (Ephesians 4:16).

3. Every member of the body shares the common life of Christ, the head (John 15:5). One part of the body cannot tell another that it is not needed, for we all need each other because we all belong together in Christ.

All the biblical pictures of the church – nation, building, body and so on – are corporate. Bricks need to be touching and bonded together; flesh needs to be attached to muscle and bone. Every picture demands some sort of organisation. Nations without government and leadership are anarchic; buildings without structure are piles of rubble; bodies without structure and leadership are floundering heaps.

Church Structure

No church can function without structure. If we were to start a church today, we would need to make arrangements for meetings and taking decisions. We would have to learn from the Scriptures and from the Spirit how to express our church life. The New Testament does not provide us with a rigid and dogmatic pattern for a perfect church structure and an ideal organisation. However it does offer several important principles. At the simplest level, these can be reduced to four which need to be applied in any church which is serious about moving towards a more biblical pattern.

United yet diverse
The New Testament body picture shows that there are many different members which each has a quite different function. Any structure must express both the body's unity of purpose and its diversity of function. There is one church, but there are many gifts. This is a fundamental principle which must be worked out in any church which aspires to follow NT principles. Somehow, the church must be co-ordinated and organised together whilst ensuring that there is ample room for a wide variety of expressions of Christ's ministry.

Equal yet distinct
Equality is very highly stressed in the New Testament. 1 Corinthians 12:22-26 and James 2:1-4 make it plain that worldly standards and status have no place in the church. Those parts of the human body which are not presentable are given greater honour, so too in the church body those who appear less important must be honoured and valued.

Some churches are adopting management structures which consider some people to be more important than others. That must not be so in a biblical church. We are all equal in the sight of God, and all equal in his body. Some men and women who have been entrusted with leadership gifts are inevitably more prominent and visible, and they have been charged with greater responsibilities. But they are not superior to the rest of the body, and they are not more important before God.

Within the equality there should be a distinction of function. Ephesians 4:11-13 and 1 Corinthians 12 4-11 show that there is one Spirit but many gifts – which he distributes at will to each individual. There is always a temptation to ascribe too much importance to one gift, or to consider one function to be over-important. 1 Corinthians 12:28-31 shows that there are higher gifts, but we must always apply Paul's 1 Corinthians 13:13 principle.

Total membership involvement

For too long, the church has been led by a professional elite. Members have thought that they were meant to support an omni-competent minister who was supposed to do everything on their behalf.

Thank God that, in recent years, the Spirit has opened our eyes to see that the ministry of the church belongs to all the saints. Leaders are meant to equip the saints for the work of ministry – not do it all for them! The growth and health of the body depend on each part functioning to capacity. We need structures which encourage this truth.

Fully flexible

It is self evident that dead bodies do not grow and change. Living organisms are always on the move. In Luke 5:37-39, Jesus taught that new wine needs new wineskins. In New Testament days, unfermented wine was put into bags made from animal skins. The wine expanded as it fermented, and the skin was flexible enough to accommodate it. When the wine had been used, the old skin could not be re-used because it had lost its flexibility – unless it was thoroughly soaked to restore its flexibility.

So too our church structures cannot contain the new life and growth of the Spirit when they are rigid and inflexible. The only way that church structures can function effectively is by being flexible enough to allow constant renewing by the Spirit.

Church Government

No church can function without government. Throughout history the church has never settled on one system of government, as the New Testament does not lay down rigid rules: once again, it offers guidelines for us to apply with the Spirit's help.

As Christ is unarguably the head of the church, the church is under his government. No single system can adequately express his rule fully. He may share his rule through one individual, through a few, or through all his people. Sovereign God is free to express his will as he chooses. It is simply up to us to listen to him as carefully as we can.

Traditionally the church has used one of four main systems of church government.

Episcopalian
In the Church of England, every parish has a church, over every church is a minister, and over every minister is a bishop. This is a hierarchical system, but it can work well when the bishops and ministers are full of God's love and passion. At its best, it guarantees that all pastors are themselves pastored properly.

Presbyterian
This is rule by a small group of elders or presbyters who have been chosen or elected by some system. It works well when the elders are in agreement and have jointly heard God's will. Its great advantage is that it is clear to all who governs the local church.

Congregational
This is democratic rule by the majority of the congregation. This

works well when a whole congregation is moved by God's power and there is a clear consensus about his will. Ideally, this reveals the important truth that Christ is in the whole body, and not just in an elite. But the majority is not always right – only two of the Canaan spies were correct.

Apostolic
This is rule by one charismatic leader who calls people to follow him and do the work of God. Again, this works well when the leader has been envisioned and anointed by God. Its strength is that there is always a clear and agreed vision. But who pastors the leader? And who takes over when he moves on?

Clearly no system is perfect, and history shows us that God has worked through them all. We must simply try to recognise his voice whether in the congregation, an outside ministry, an individual or a group of elders. It seems to me that six NT principles need to be kept in mind whenever church government is considered.

1. Christ is the one and only head. He is the ultimate church leader.

2. There are a variety of leadership gifts which are not vested in one omni-competent individual.

3. Christ is himself present in all the members – each member can hear God for themselves through the Spirit.

4. Jesus came not to be served but to serve, and he set an example of foot-washing for his under-leaders to follow. Authoritarian or coercive patterns of government should be absent.

5. Every expression of the church has integrity and is a valid unit.

6. Every expression of the church should be interdependent and co-dependent with all other local expressions – and in some relationship with wider expressions of the world-wide body.

Church Leadership

No church can function without leaders and leadership. Jesus is the leader of the church. He governs and directs his church through his word and through his Spirit. Whatever our role in the church, we have to submit to Christ's headship.

When we submit to Christ we are submitting to each other, as all are equally joined to Christ. Ephesians 5:21 teaches that we all are subject to each other – because we acknowledge Christ in each other. This means that leadership is not a few ruling the many, but all serving each other in a variety of ways – of which leadership is only one.

Local Leadership

The New Testament church had a basic two-fold leadership pattern consisting of elders and deacons (Philippians 1:1).

Elders
Elders were called and equipped by the Spirit to care for God's flock. In the New Testament, they were involved in visiting and healing the sick (James 5:14); teaching God's word and Christian doctrine (1 Timothy 5:17); receiving gifts on behalf of the community (Acts 11:30); and recognising and laying hands on gifted members.

Their primary task was the general oversight of the local congregation (1 Peter 5:2); but they also took part in wider church councils (Acts 15:4-6,23; 16:4). Paul and Barnabas ordained elders in all the Asian churches (Acts 14:23), and Paul encouraged Titus to do the same in Crete (Titus 1:5). 1 Timothy 3:1-7 and Titus 1:5-9 indicate the qualities elders should possess.

Most elders seem to have been of equal rank and they appear to have acted corporately – as in 1 Timothy 4:14 where the body of elders ordained Timothy. However, 1 Timothy 3:1 refers to a 'presiding elder', Acts 15:5-21 indicates that James was the senior elder in Jerusalem – a 'first among equals' – with the final responsibility before God, John describes himself in 2 John 1 and

3 John 1 as 'The Elder'. It has been put that elders are called to govern by 'guarding, guiding and grazing'. That is to guard the flock from the enemy, to guide the people along the ways of God, and to graze the members by teaching and preaching.

Deacons

Deacons were called and equipped to assist the elders in all the practical and serving details so that the elders could apply themselves fully to the work of spiritual oversight.

The Greek word *diakonos* means servant or waiter and is often used in the New Testament for waiting at tables (Mark 1:31; Luke 10:40). Interestingly, Jesus introduces himself as The Deacon in Luke 22:26 in the context of waiting at table. *Diakanos* is also used in relation to general practical ministry in Romans 15:25 and 2 Corinthians 8:4, and to those who help Paul practically in Acts 19:22; Philemon 13; Colossians 4:7 and Ephesians 6:21.

In Romans 12:7 and 1 Peter 4:11, serving, *diakonia*, is named as a special gift from God. It is on a par with prophecy and ruling, and is meant to be exercised by those who have received this gift from God. It is usually inferred that the Spirit-filled men of Acts 6 were the first deacons – though they are not named as such. They had the responsibility of administering the widows' fund, and of releasing the apostles for the ministry of the word.

1 Timothy 3:8-11 describes the character of deacons, and 1 Timothy 3:11 seems to describe female deacons (or deaconesses): certainly Phoebe is named as a deaconess in Romans 16:1.

Titles are not so important, what matters most is that the biblical leadership functions are being fulfilled. Local churches need not have elders and deacons, so long as there is an identifiable leadership doing these jobs.

Trans-Local Leadership

Each New Testament local church had its own leadership and was responsible directly to Christ, the head of the church. In Revelation, there is a different message from him to each church in Asia Minor. Christ had a specific word for each church, but these messages were to be heard by all the other churches; which is why Jesus says, 'hear what the Spirit says to the *churches*' (Revelation 2:7,11,17,29; 3:6,13,22).

This re-enforces the fact that every local church is only one expression of the body – we cannot break away from each other; there must be relationship between churches. I believe that one of the best ways of maintaining these relationships is by recognising ministries at a trans-local level. This means that we receive ministries which are God's gift to the body even though they are based in a different fellowship – or even another country. That is precisely what we see in Revelation chapters 1-3, where each church in Asia Minor had its own local leadership, but recognised and benefited from John's wider ministry.

I believe that *all* the ministries listed in Ephesians 4:11 should be rooted in local churches where they should work alongside the elders (Acts 15:6,22). However, it seems that these Ephesians 4:11 ministries also have a trans-local function.

I believe that biblical local churches are governed by elders – some of whom will also probably be apostles, prophets, evangelists, pastors and teachers – and that eldership is a purely local ministry. Within local churches, however, those with an Ephesians 4:11 gifting can express their ministry both through their local church (as part of the local elders) and beyond it in other churches where they are welcomed by those churches' elders and – like Paul in Acts 21:17-25 – submit to those elders.

Apostles

Apostles are those who are sent or commissioned. In the New Testament there are at least three types of apostles [i] Jesus Christ, [ii] the foundation apostles, and [iii] general apostles.

Foundation apostles were chosen by Christ as special eye witnesses who had been with him from the start. They had unique and unrepeatable qualifications. They had special authority to witness and pass on Christ's teaching. Obviously they belonged only to the first generation of believers.

Some leaders teach that foundation apostles were the only

apostles. But the New Testament also names Barnabas, Andronicus and Junias (probably a woman) as apostles. Ephesians 4:11 indicates that all the giftings are to build up the church *until* it is fully mature. This will not be attained until Jesus returns. It seems, therefore, that apostles are necessary for building and equipping the saints in every age and place until the end of time.

The first apostles were sent ahead of Jesus to the places he would be visiting, and general apostles also are always pioneers who are sent ahead to spearhead the work of the gospel. They demonstrate the presence of God by their actions and preaching. They earn the right of the church to be heard. Apostles may be unpopular, many of them have had to lay down their lives, but they are the people who establish new Christian communities.

Prophets

Prophets are called to live in close communion with God. They enter his presence to hear his thoughts, and emerge to preach, to encourage, to explain what God is doing, or to challenge the standards and behaviour of the church and the world. Ideally, they pass on only what God is thinking and doing, and do not taint the message with their own opinions, attitudes and cultural values.

In the New Testament, there appear to have been two types of prophets. There were those who functioned only within a local church – where all people were always encouraged to seek God for prophecy. And there were those – like Agabus – who were recognised more widely and functioned trans-locally: these are the prophets referred to in Ephesians 4:11.

The New Testament ministry of prophet involves at least seven principles:

1. It was officially recognised. Men or women whom a local church recognised over a period of time as regularly receiving and passing on prophecies were recognised as prophets. They were not appointed to a position; they had proved to have a share in Christ's ministry.

2. Their ministry was one of factual revelation (Acts 11:27-30; 13:1-3).

3. They spoke by the inspiration of the Holy Spirit (Acts 11:27).

4. They were not infallible. Agabus' prophecy in Acts 21:10 was broadly accurate, but some of the details did not occur exactly as he had prophesied. This did not nullify the thrust of his message – which was true. Even so, Paul did not act on the message; instead he used it to prepare himself for the coming ordeal! This shows that we have a serious duty to 'weigh'/'sift'/'assess' prophecy.

5. They sometimes predicted the future (Acts 11:27-30).

6. They gave direction for ministry which confirmed what people already knew (Acts 13:11-3; 1 Timothy 1:18, 4:14; 2 Timothy 1:6).

7. They pointed to what God was doing (Acts 11:27-30). Agabus did not demand a human response; he simply warned of a coming famine and left it to the people to respond practically as they were led. The trans-local prophet passed on God's word, and the local leaders decided how the prophecy should be acted upon. Like Genesis 41, this was real famine relief, providing before the shortage occurred!

Evangelists
The word *evangelist* comes from the verb *euangelizomai* which means 'to announce the good news'. The verb is very common in the New Testament, but the title 'evangelist' appears only three times. In 2 Timothy 4:5, Timothy is urged to do the work of an evangelist. In Acts 21:8, Philip is described as 'the evangelist'. And the office is listed as a special gift to the church in Ephesians 4:11.

Although all Christians are called 'to announce the good news', there are those with a special gifting in evangelism. The only two evangelists mentioned in the New Testament, Philip and Timothy, both had local and trans-local ministries. Acts describes Philip's travels in Samaria before settling in Caesarea. And Timothy travelled with Paul before settling in Ephesus.

Pastors and teachers

Pastors and teachers are often closely related ministries, and perform an indispensable function. Together they build on the foundations laid down by apostles, prophets and evangelists. Usually they stay in one place, often for many years, caring for the church. They teach it the word of God and the ways of Jesus, establish it on scriptural foundations, and emphasise its essential unity with all Christians down the centuries, through the traditions and across the world.

However, pastors and teachers also have a vital trans-local function. Those with a special gifting in teaching are often called to travel widely – especially to teach other teachers. And those with a special pastoral gifting can offer pastoral help to those pastors and leaders who are not themselves being pastored because of their church government structure.

In Ephesians 4:12, Paul shows that all these ministries were given by Jesus to prepare the church for service. And the Greek word he uses, *diakonia*, means practical, menial, foot-washing, table-waiting service. Each individual believer is meant to serve God, other disciples and the world. But the four categories of leaders are meant to ensure that the church as a whole is characterised by this sort of humble service.

Church Functions

We have seen that Christ gave his church the responsibility of making, mobilising and maturing disciples. It seems to me that this calling involves functioning in five different areas, and all five are necessary if the church is to have a complete and balanced ministry. They inter-relate, overlap and affect each other greatly, but any church which aspires to be biblical will ensure that it functions effectively in *all* five areas.

Worship
The supreme all-embracing call of the one church is to worship God. Whenever we come together we are called to worship the Father, to acknowledge him for who he is – the Creator and Redeemer of the whole world. We should long to worship Jesus for who he is – the eternal Son and Saviour of all humanity. And we should honour the Holy Spirit – our enabler and encourager.

John 4:23-24 shows that the Father wants us to worship him in Spirit and in truth. He is not much concerned with our musical tastes, but he aches for our hearts and minds to be right before him. We must make sure that our church worship is significant, meaningful, skilful and culturally relevant. God does not want our worship to be dull, repetitive or boring. He wants us to worship him creatively, in fresh, exciting ways which reflect his own creative nature.

Worship is important because we find God there. He reveals himself in worship and '*is enthroned on the praises of his people*'. Many spiritual breakthroughs come in worship, and we need to work hard to ensure that we offer God the best from our culture.

Word
The church is the custodian of eternal truth – the written word of God. Across the world, there are many rival claims to the truth; and, in Europe, we live in a post-modern culture which denies even the concept of absolute truth. Therefore we need to teach and preach the truth with the greatest possible care and clarity. It is of the utmost importance, today, that we maintain our devotion to God's word. All sorts of emphases and fashions can distract us from scripture. But the word must remain primary.

Every aspect of church life must be rooted in scripture. Every ministry must be based in biblical principles. Every believer needs constant encouragement to subordinate his thinking to God's word. New converts are increasingly coming into the church with no biblical background and a great mass of human ideas. So it is urgent that they are quickly taught the eternal principles of grace and faith.

Witness

The work of the church is witness. We are called to be his witnesses – in word and deed and lifestyle. The church explodes with growth when people are equipped and released as witnesses. Churches which do not burn with a passion for mission are missing the whole point of their calling – to go and make disciples. Too many churches seem to think that Jesus charged them with holding meetings and waiting for people to come to them. But the church is called to go...

Of course, we need the guidance of the Spirit to find appropriate ways of witnessing which will reach our generation and culture. But, ultimately, the most effective witnesses are believers who live the ordinary dedicated life of Jesus, and gossip the good news in language that the people around them understand.

Welfare

Some churches are so evangelistic that they ignore pastoral care, and others do the reverse. We must find a balance and ensure that the people in our churches are properly pastored. This does not just mean a visit when someone is ill or bereaved; it may mean practical caring as in Acts 6. In fact it was the practical caring of the early church which made it so dynamically attractive!

We are also called to care for the welfare of the community around us as well. We must not neglect community care. Jesus calls us to serve with him. This must be a major emphasis of the church – especially as society disintegrates and social needs multiply. It is no coincidence that revivals have often occurred when the church has been deeply involved with social needs.

We do not serve people as a means to the end of preaching to them – our welfare must be a genuine outpouring of Christ's love. But if we take care of the sick, the elderly, the broken-hearted, the imprisoned, the strangers and foreigners, the homeless and so on, people will know that Jesus is alive and living in his church. And they will seek him out.

Warfare

Matthew 16:18 states that the gates of Hades will not prevail against the church. This presupposes that the church will be involved with warfare. We will not be able to do the work of Jesus without grappling with the spiritual forces opposed to God's kingdom.

But we have been ordered to trample the enemy underfoot, not to inspect his squashed corpse with a magnifying glass. We are interested in Christology, not demonology! We do need to confront demonic powers through prayer, fasting and praise, but we need to do it cautiously, under the direction of the Spirit – not rashly, five times in every meeting! Warfare prayer is on God's agenda, but we must be clearly guided by the Spirit and directed by the Lord in everything we do.

4

On To
Maturity

Ephesians 4 is one of the great biblical chapters, and we have returned to it time and again in this booklet. It contains a snapshot view of a wonderful heavenly vision – the glorious end-time church.

Jesus promises that he will complete what he began so long ago. He will establish a biblical church. He has been working on it throughout history, right until now – the most exciting period yet in church history. When Jesus returns for his bride, he will not come for an infant church but for a mature bride. He has promised that he will build his church, and this means he will complete his task.

As Christ's body, the church is God's agent or representative in the world. Christ's work on earth can only be carried out through his body. When it is not a mature, strong and healthy body, the work of Christ is not done. But when the body is strong, and growing towards maturity, then God's work on earth can be accomplished.

In Ephesians 4:11-16, Paul writes about the church attaining the fullness of Christ. This means that, one day, the church will perfectly reveal Christ in all his fullness right here *on earth.* This stresses Paul's teaching in Ephesians 1:23, where he describes the church as 'the fullness of him' ".

Paul makes it plain that Jesus has given apostles, prophets, evangelists, pastors and teachers to the church so that they will knit all God's people together for the work of service. It is this which builds up Christ's body. According to Paul, these leaders are to go on with their work, building up the church, until four wonderful things occur.

Unity

First, Paul promises that the mature church will reach the unity of the faith. This is not the unity of the Spirit which began at the cross and already exists, but unity in the essential doctrines of the faith and a mature understanding of Christ. This does not mean that all Christians will believe exactly the same things about everything, but rather that there will be strong unity in all the essentials of the faith throughout the whole church.

That may seem hard to believe. But when I reflect on the changes in the church in the last thirty years – and consider the advances in trans-denominational and trans-traditional links – I can see how Christ is uniting his church in the faith. And I can believe that the unity Paul describes is not so very far away..

Full knowledge

Secondly, Paul asserts that the mature church will reach a full knowledge of the Son of God. This is not just an improved version of our current knowledge; it is *full* knowledge.

In Philippians 3:8-16, Paul longs to know Christ – and the power of his resurrection, and the depth of his sufferings. And in Philippians 2:5-11, he urges us to make the mind of Christ our own. He offers a roller-coaster description of the Son of God who emptied himself, took the form of a slave, accepted death – and was raised so high that all beings everywhere should bend the knee to him.

When the church moves beyond wanting power for its own sake and longs to think and be like the serving Jesus; when we yearn to share both his power *and* his suffering; then we will be beginning to rise towards this full knowledge of the Son. Sometime soon, the biblical church will experience his full reality in every area of their church life.

Full stature

Thirdly, the mature church will form the perfect Man; we will be of full stature, fully mature. No longer will we be children, tossed one way or another, but strong and mature in Christ. The church is not dying out. It is not fading away. It is coming of age.

The church we read about in Acts is the infant church. The end-time church will be a mature, adult, vigorous church. If the early church was able to achieve so much, what will the end-time church accomplish? I am sure that the coming biblical church will see a massive outpouring of the Spirit which will lead to effective world-wide evangelism.

Christ's fullness

And fourthly, the mature church will be filled with the fullness of Christ himself. This means that we will be so full of Jesus that we can accurately represent him in the world and achieve everything he has asked.

This biblical, mature church will be full of his power, his wisdom, his love and his authority. It will show the world the fullness of his grace and holiness. Christ will be fully manifest both in us and through us.

The full church will be body of credible active witnesses throughout the entire world, in every nation and culture. This is a vision worth working towards, a dream worth living for. Even the smallest step taken towards a more biblical church will be extremely valuable.

In this little booklet, I've tried to set down the main biblical principles about the church that I can see in the New Testament. I do not think that anything is more precious to Christ than the health of his bride, and I pray that you will sift through my words to find the solid gold of scripture. When you are sure that you understand God's principles for his church, please begin to apply them in your situation. I urge you to find the courage to move away from the shallow waters of your particular church tradition. Let go and swim with Jesus in the raging torrent of living waters which is eternal life in the Spirit.

I promise you that, if we live by the truth and in love, we shall grow completely into Christ – who is the head by whom the whole body is fitted and joined together, every joint adding its own strength for each individual part to work according to its function.

So the body grows, until it has built itself up in love.

If you have enjoyed this book and would like to help us to send a copy of it and many other titles to needy pastors in the **Third World**, please write for further information or send your gift to:

Sovereign World Trust, P.O. Box 777, Tonbridge, Kent TN11 9XT, United Kingdom

or to the **'Sovereign World'** distributor in your country. If sending money from outside the United Kingdom, please send an International Money Order or Foreign Bank Draft in STERLING, drawn on a **UK** bank to **Sovereign World Trust**.